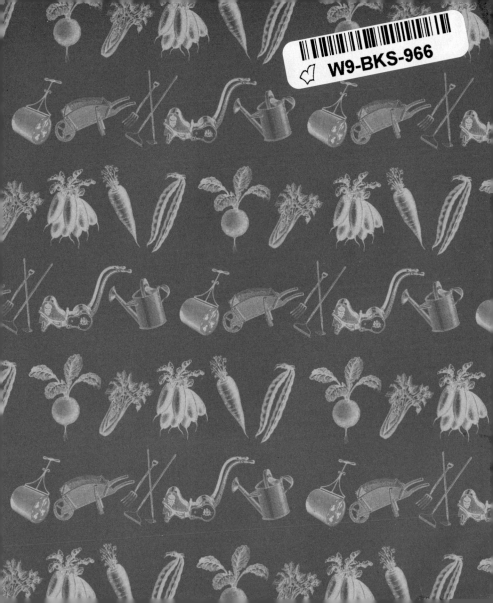

Tips from the
OLD GARDENERS

"As is the gardener, so is the garden."

Duncan Crosbie

CONARI PRESS

First published in 2005 by Conari Press,
an imprint of Red Wheel/Weiser, LLC
York Beach, ME
With offices at:
368 Congress Street
Boston, MA 02210
www.redwheelweiser.com

Library of Congress Cataloging-in-Publication Data available upon request.

ISBN: 1-57324-219-5

Printed in China

12 11
9 8 7 6 5 4 3

Contents

Foreword   5

Were the old wives telling tales?   7
A quick look at some old folklore

I'll be nice to you if you're nice to me   11
Planting and sowing

Don't you want to grow up nice and strong?   23
Stimulating growth

How to make friends and influence plants   34
Protecting your plants

Will no one rid me of this turbulent bug?   48
Tips on pest control

The next round's on me!   72
Encouraging friends into the garden

What have you got? Well don't come near me then   77
Some plants that heal

"*A garden is a grand teacher. It teaches patience and careful watchfulness; industry and thrift; above all, entire trust.*"

Gertrude Jekyll
1843–1932

Foreword

The Romans never travelled anywhere without a chestful or two of herbal plants, and since they marched over most of Europe in their time we have more to thank them for than straight roads alone. Many of the plants they brought came from southern Europe but they also brought the tradition of their uses from ancient Egypt.

When the Romans departed in the 5th century, it was the monasteries that kept alive the herbal lore they left behind, steadily adding to it by trial, error and careful observation. From early mediaeval times the monks and nuns had both kitchen gardens, for their food, and physic gardens for healing herbs – as devotees of the *Brother Cadfael* novels and television series will know. The wisdom they developed in the matter of growing and using plants was the origin of our gardening traditions.

For cottagers and ordinary rural dwellers, though, gardens were a strictly practical undertaking. Before the beginnings of the Industrial Revolution we lived in an agrarian economy. Our very survival depended on our skills in growing plants for food and healing. Crop failure, whether through disease or bad weather, could mean death by starvation and even in good years the diets of many barely stretched to survival levels. Acute observation of what worked and what did not and the handing on of accumulated knowledge was essential to existence. Gardens as a source of pleasure began in the 16th century as the landed gentry gradually acquired greater leisure; and as the great gardens of the 19th century were developed, the hundreds of gardeners they employed inherited this knowledge and developed it further. Although some of it was written down, much of this folk wisdom was passed on by word of mouth, being added to all the time.

Occasionally it is pure superstition or wishful thinking (for example, *if your rake falls prongs upward it will rain the next day*), but mostly it is sound and practical. For a while in the 20th century, as science progressed ever faster, we derided folklore and traditional remedies. Now, we are less trustful of purely chemical solutions fearing the side effects of some of the toxins used. Yet many plants contain toxins as well as beneficial properties and, ironically perhaps, science has been able to demonstrate that much folklore, including that about the uses of such plants, is accurate.

Nearly all of us nowadays garden purely for pleasure, most of us in smallish gardens. This little book does not pretend to be a solemn guide to all gardening folklore, but only to pass on – with a moderately straight face – some of the old gardening folk wisdom in the hope that bits of it, at least, might prove useful for you.

Were the old wives telling tales?
A quick look at some old folklore

Always grow some herbs outside the herb garden.

What an absurd idea. A herb garden is for herbs, so a flower garden is for flowers and a veggie garden for vegetables, isn't it? That, at least, is how the severely logical modern mind is likely to react. We are used to everything being where we want and expect to find it. We don't go shopping expecting to buy bread at the chemists, or fruit in the hardware shop, so why, for goodness sake, scatter herbs around outside the herb garden?

There is a reason, and a very practical one. To our grandparents and our more distant ancestors, the garden was the source of food and medicine. They had a lot less wealth and leisure than nearly all of us have today, and it was a practical necessity to get it right when it came to gardening. Gardening folklore – old wives tales – was of no use to them if it didn't provide useful guidance, so although a lot of it may sound illogical, and occasionally farcical, to us, it often turns out to be a mixture of common sense and practical experience.

So why should we grow a few herbs outside the herb garden, then? Because many plants classified as herbs contain natural chemicals that either encourage growth in other plants or protect them against pests and disease.

For example, cabbages planted around with sage, thyme or rosemary do well; borage helps strawberries thrive; pot marigolds secrete an insect repellent that protects many surrounding plants; parsley encourages bees and also protects asparagus, beans and carrots; and so on. That's why, in the old cottage garden, things often appeared haphazard with different plants or herbs or vegetables scattered here or there apparently — but not in fact — at random. When you know the reason, it's perfectly straightforward.

If you want to know when to sow, take your trousers off and sit on the ground!

This is my favourite old wives tale, and another one that is senseless at first sight. All it meant, in days before we acquired sophisticated means for measuring soil temperature, was that feeling the bare soil with one's tender flesh was a good – if uncomfortable - way of finding out if it was warm enough to start the spring planting.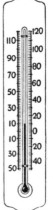

By late Victorian times, this was thought of as not nice at all. No doubt visitors to the local great estate were disconcerted by the sight of under-gardeners sitting bare-bottomed in the kitchen garden sporting nothing but a quizzical look upon their weathered faces. So a p.c. version of the folklore was hastily invented, and it became permissible – indeed expected – that the temperature of the soil could be judged using your elbow. In today's permissive climate, I would not dream of recommending which way is right for you!

This concern with the effects of climate reminds us how important weather was to olden day gardeners. There is much folklore, all of it gloomy, about the weather. For example: *If on the eighth of June it rain, that foretells a wet harvest.* Not exactly a bundle of optimism.

Oak before ash, we're in for a splash.
Ash before oak we're in for a soak.

Or to put it another way, whichever tree comes into leaf first, you're going to get wet.

If the first of July be rainy weather, it will rain for four weeks together; and if you escape July 1st, then July 15th lay in wait: *St Swithin's Day if thou dost rain, for forty days it will remain* (in other words until August 24th). But lo and behold! Modern meteorologists studying weather history have found that there is truth in the saying. The weather of mid July sets a pattern that does indeed last until about August 24th, St Bartholomew's Day. But don't get excited, because:

If it rains on St Bartholomew's Day
It will rain for forty more, they say!

I'll be nice to you if you're nice to me
Planting and sowing

When it comes to sowing seeds gardening lore has many variations about how thickly to sow, but they add up to the same advice:

> *Plant your seeds in a row,*
> *one for the pheasant, one for the crow,*
> *one to rot and one to grow.*

> or

> *Sow seed generously*
> *one for the rook, one for the crow,*
> *one to die and one to grow*

In short, err on the generous side. Between seed predators and natural failure they're not all going to germinate satisfactorily. And if you're lucky and they do, you should prick out the unwanted seedlings to avoid overcrowding.

Long ago they used to say that to *"keep byrdes, antes and mice away from seeds"* you should *"sprinkle them first with juice of houseleek"*.

By all means. But it's quicker and easier to roll them in a paraffin-damped cloth before sowing, and especially good for broad beans. Little pieces of gorse stuck in the seed rows also helps to deter mice, who don't like a prick in a tender place any more than we do.

Sow beans in the mud,
they'll grow like wood.
and
The rule in gardening, never forget,
to sow dry and set wet.

Gardeners are prone to head shaking and pursed lips on the subject of when to sow. These warnings mean be sure the cold, wet phase of spring weather has passed, and the ground is beginning its warming up process, before you sow your seeds. But exactly when that may be depends on the climate where you live, as well as the type of soil in your garden.

If you live in an area of high rainfall, or if you are in the north where the spring warmth comes a week or two later, one solution could be to give your peas and broad beans a good start by sowing them in pots, planting them out when the ground outside is warmer and drier. Seeds can be sown in trays and kept in a greenhouse or on a window ledge and transplanted – after hardening off – when a few inches tall. But another saying is *who sows in May gets little that way*. In other words, don't be overcautious, or you may leave it too late.

"Set wet" is a tip for setting your beans, especially runner beans, by watering the flowers – these days playing a sprinkler hose over them saves time. But in a typical British summer you can often leave the rain to do the job for you!

Never sow seeds when the moon is waning

There's an old wives tale if ever I heard one.

Or is it? Apparently not. Scientific research has come up with corroboration of old folk wisdom.

Lunar fluctuations affect Earth's magnetic field, and its atmosphere, causing all water, including that in even the smallest living organism, to move in almost tidal fashion. This makes significant rainfall statistically more likely after a new moon. So if you sow your seeds (once the earth has benefited from spring warming, of course) after the full moon, they should get a good shower or two to help their germination. This is a piece of observation that goes all the way back to the ancient Egyptians.

If science can prove the wisdom of that old wives tale, perhaps it could next examine this one: *Radishes pulled up as the moon wanes will cure corns and warts.*

There's a fortune waiting to be made!

Giving your seeds a hot shower

When I was a youngster, I was taught to pour hot water into the empty seed drill immediately before putting the seeds in. Others will say cover the seeds first, then put hot water in a can with a fine rose and sprinkle it along the drill. A refinement is to follow this up an hour later with a sprinkling of lukewarm water. The point of all this tender loving care is, of course, to give the seeds a good start in life by encouraging early germination. And it works – usually.

What beans like best

Beans love plenty of good, cool moisture at their roots. This doesn't mean sowing them in mud, as we've already seen, but as the weather gets warmer and drier they'll repay you for ensuring that they're in moisture retentive soil. One way to help them achieve this is to put a layer or two of newspaper under them in the bottom of the trench along with some manure or compost. If you want to hear your beans purring, then see if you can find some hair to add. Human or horse hair, it doesn't matter. Beans want a rich soil and hair contains valuable minerals.

Tips from the
OLD GARDENERS

Fuschias love bracken

And not just fuschias. Except for the lime loving ones, most plants will benefit from a handful of chopped bracken at the bottom of the hole beneath a new planting. It should be green, not brown, dying bracken, and it will encourage root growth by retaining moisture.

When you hear the cuckoo shout,
'tis time to plant your tatties out.

I was brought up on the belief that Good Friday is the day to put the potatoes in. Since Good Friday can vary by four or five weeks from one year to another that's about as exact as the old saying

about the cuckoo, whose first call might be heard any time from mid March to early May.

The best that can be said is that you won't go too far wrong in about the second week of April — but just as with the sowing of seeds, allow for the variation in climate in your part of the country.

16

Make sure you've got mothballs in the cupboard

Mothballs keep cropping up in gardening because they contain naphthalene or camphor and there are insects and animals that can't stand them. When you're putting your potato tubers in, pop a mothball in next to each one and the slugs will turn tail and look for something else to eat. The tuber won't be affected. One word of warning though. Ask for the old mothballs. The more modern ones are made of chemical substitutes and don't have the same effect.

Mothballs are also on the carrot fly's no-go list, so another tip is to crumble a few mothballs into the soil around your carrot drills, and then water with a fine rose to help wash the mothball particles well in.

Crop rotation

The old herbalists wagged many a monastic finger at their novices in advising them never to plant a herb in the same place twice. They were the early advocates of the generally sound principle of crop rotation in the vegetable garden, which has two benefits.

Different plants take a different mix of nutrients from the soil, so the same crop repeatedly in the same place will exhaust the soil of the nutrients it needs for success. A secondary point is that pests feeding on a particular plant will take up permanent residence if you are kind enough to present them with their meal in the same place each year.

Obviously in a small garden crop rotation is less easy to practice. If you are fond of growing the same vegetables each year, you will need to find out which nutrients you need to replace. Modern garden centres have a wide range of fertilisers, with contents listed, so you can replenish your soil as necessary. Growbags are a good alternative for vegetables with a root system other than *umbelliferae* (carrots, parsnips etc).

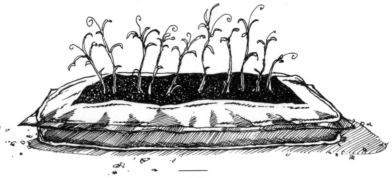

Plant in the evening, not the morning

If you are transplanting, or putting in new plants from the nursery, a good rule of thumb is to enjoy your afternoon tea first, then do it. This is just because the heat of the day is waning by then, and in those important first few hours the roots can enjoy the warmth of the soil without the leaves being scorched by the sun.

Apples, pears, hawthorn, oak:
Set them at All-Hallows-Tide, and command them to
*   prosper;*
Set them at Candlemas and entreat them to grow.

It sounds like ancient mysticism, but it's really very practical and straightforward. The autumn – before November 1st (*All Saints Day*) – is a good time to plant new trees (and most shrubs) because the ground has retained warmth from the summer and this encourages the roots to make growth and get established before the tree or shrub shuts down for the winter. Conversely, the ground takes time to warm up again in the new year and planting too early (*before Candlemas, February 2nd*) will not produce the same benefit (indeed many would say February and March is still on the early side).

Moving an established plant

Of course, the best advice is don't do it. You'd be pretty miffed if someone came along and dragged you out of your house and dumped you in some other place you hadn't chosen, and would probably have a good long sulk at the very least. Certain plants, notably peonies and dicentras (bleeding heart in particular) rarely recover from the indignity of being bundled out of their beds. But on the whole plants are remarkably accommodating provided you show a little thoughtfulness and TLC in effecting the upheaval.

Using a fork rather than a spade, which will cut too many roots, loosen the soil at a good distance from the main stem all round the plant. A good distance would be about three inches for small plants like petunias and primulas, and proportionately further out the larger the plant. Water it well before you lift it, and next prepare a hole of the same depth, but twice as wide, as the hole you've just dug round the plant you're moving. Plants don't like to have their roots constricted any more than you like squeezing into a jacket two sizes too small, so the object is to make sure the receiving hole has plenty of room for the roots to spread outwards.

If the plant is small, you can lift it in cupped hands, being sure to keep as much soil round the roots as possible. If it is larger, lift it into sacking or polythene and tie it securely round the root ball before moving to the new home. When you've settled it into the new hole, spread the roots as much as you can without breaking the root ball away, then water it well and let the water soak away before filling in the hole and firming the ground well. But plants need some air at the root so if your soil is heavy clay, or if it's wet, don't firm the ground too vigorously or you'll drive out *all* the air.

"The first step in getting to know a plant intimately is to dig it up and study it's root system. Learn how it eats and drinks. See how far it forages for food. Know your root and garden wisdom will be added unto you."

Richard Wright

1933

Don't you want to grow up nice and strong?
Stimulating growth

Unusual things to help plants grow

Banana skins and dripping: **Roses love it if you dig in old banana skins just beneath the surface of the soil around their roots. The skins contain a long list of goodies – phosphates, calcium, sulphur, silica, sodium and magnesium – in which many soils are deficient.**

If you're putting in new roses (don't laugh, this is serious) bury a good wedge of cooking lard beneath the roots. My father was addicted to dripping, but if we could prise it away from him, this too went under the roses. (It did the roses a lot more good than it did him, but he didn't see it that way at all.) The roses will show their appreciation when they come into bloom.

23

Tips from the
OLD GARDENERS

Beer: It may be hard to accept, but humans are not the only ones to like beer. Most vegetables appreciate a drop now and again, but it's the *brassicas* that are the old soaks. Cabbages in particular like to have a regular drink - say once a week. And it's not just cabbages that will make inroads to your beer supplies. It's an excellent liquid food for flowers as well, especially the tall ones such as delphiniums and hollyhocks. But at least they can't come rolling home singing rude songs and clinging to the door post.

Milk: When the milk bottle or container is empty fill it with water and shake it up well. You've then got a very mild liquid manure which you can use on your house plants or on plants and climbers growing against the walls of your house. You won't need to walk far to rinse out the milk bottles and since plants which grow near walls get less moisture than others they'll be grateful to you.

Tea Leaves: Used tea leaves are a good addition to the compost heap at all times, but azaleas, rhododendrons and camellias respond well to them as a mulch. Cold tea is equally acceptable, so whatever you have left in the pot, why not offer it to them instead of tipping it down the sink?

Nettles: No worthwhile garden should be without a good big clump of nettles. Yes, really. The benefits of nettles will crop up several times in this book, because they take and store nutrients from the soil retaining nitrogen, phosphate, iron, protein and silica. If you use nettles as a fertiliser, you'll be returning all this goodness to the soil, and many a plant will be smacking its roots in anticipation as it sees you coming with a nice canful of liquid nettle manure.

All you have to do is fill a container with rainwater and let the nettles you've cut or pulled up soak in it for a month. Then dilute what remains with more rainwater in a ratio of 1:10 and use as a liquid manure to be poured round the roots.

Nettles make a wonderful ingredient in the compost heap for the reasons given and, like any really useful plant, they also serve as a deterrent to some insects. Again, soak nettles in water but this time only for a few days, and then use the water as a spray against aphids.

Finally, there's a time-honoured tip that you should plant currant bushes in old nettle beds, or let nettles grow between the bushes. By now you will not be surprised to learn that this allows the bushes to share some of the nettles' nutrients, but also strengthens their disease resistance.

Old shoes: Leather is full of nutrients and if you've no better use for your old shoes when you've finished with them, strip off any rubber soles, plastic attachments, buckles, etc and bury them in the garden to rot down. This will take time. Since it's irritating to keep bringing them to the surface when you're forking the border (and could be embarrassing if you've just persuaded mother-in-law to lend a hand in the garden) it might be best to reserve the old boots for the bottom of the hole when you're planting a new tree or large shrub. Once on a time, in fact, old shoes were particularly recommended as food for peach trees.

Bones: If you don't keep a dog, old bones dug into the soil are also an excellent source of nutrients, but best in a dry soil with vegetables and fruit trees or bushes. If you do keep a dog, you'll either need him or her to sign a pledge of abstinence (lest your garden is reduced to an interesting landscape of hillocks and holes) or you can use bone meal, readily available from any garden centre.

Bone meal, incidentally, is said to be a great help in controlling moss in lawns. Rake out the moss first, then sprinkle bone meal over the affected areas. But beware. The dog likes that too!

Manures and composts: If you keep chickens let them run around under the fruit trees is an old piece of lore. Chicken manure is very helpful to fruit trees, especially plums, which is why

chickens were often allowed to roam loose in the orchard. But although it's difficult to credit the gormless chicken with packing a punch, its manure is strong stuff for the general garden and needs to be mixed with dry soil before being used if it's not to damage more tender plants.

Horse manure, well mixed with straw, is excellent in heavy ground containing clay, which it also helps to break up; whereas cow or pig manure is better in lighter, sandier soils. Cow dung is slower acting than horse but its effects last longer; whereas pig dung contains more nitrogen and needs mixing with earth or litter before being used for vegetables, for which it's then excellent.

If you're still reading, and haven't given up in disgust at all this talk of smelly things, it's worth adding that a time-honoured method of making a rich liquid fertiliser is to fill an old sack with manure and hang it in a barrel of water for three or four days. The liquid can then be fed to your plants with a watering can.

Leafmould: whereas animals produce manure with cheerful regularity mixed, no doubt, with a certain amount of relief, leafmould requires a lot of patience, but with the advantage of not being smelly. It's also very good for enriching dry, stony soil. Fill a large black polythene bag with your fallen leaves in the autumn, make a few small holes in the bag, fold over the top and seal it with a brick or an old paving stone, and you have nothing more to do for the next six to nine months, by which time it should have decomposed thoroughly and be ready to use.

Potash (bonfire) manure: If you live in an area where it's still possible to have a bonfire, the ash from your burned garden waste is a good substitute for animal manure.

The snag, I'm afraid, is that you need to keep the ash somewhere dry for about a year before it's ready for use! So unless you're running a country estate – in which case you are unlikely to need this book – it seems unlikely that you'll pursue the idea of potash manure any further. But just in case you do, be careful that you've not thrown any chemicals or household waste, such as plastics, on the fire. If you haven't, you can put the ash in the compost heap and let it rot down along with all the other things in it.

Don't pull up the roots of beans and peas.

When you've had your fill of beans and peas and they have nothing left to give, they leave a straggly, untidy mess behind. It's very tempting to pull the whole lot up, keep the growing frame or sticks for next year, and chuck the rest on the bonfire or compost heap. But hang on a minute!

Those little white globs, a bit like small boils, that you see on the roots are not some unmentionable fungus or the handiwork of malicious but unidentified insects. They are storage pods for valuable nitrates which will do your soil no end of good if you leave them in peace to get on with it. So by all means tidy up the bean and pea patch by cutting off the tops just above the soil, but leave the roots where they are to enjoy the winter unmolested, and they'll repay you by replenishing your soil in time for next season.

Making your own compost container: With a roll of chicken wire and four or six old posts, you can easily make a square or circular container to make leafmould or compost, and use a bit of old carpet trimmed to size as a lid. You'll need to remember to use galvanised wire and nails or staples to prevent rusting, of course.

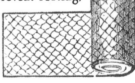

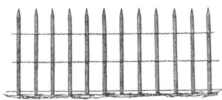

Alternatively, if you belong to that tiny percentage of the population that just happens to be tearing up old floorboards as you read this, you could save yourself a trip to the local dump and make yourself an up-market compost container by nailing the old floorboards, sawn to the size you want, to upright posts. The clever thing would be to make the front removable since, with the normal unfairness of life in general, the good compost is always at the bottom. You could do this by making a hinged front, with a hook and eye to keep it closed. Or if your carpentry skills are of the kind I can only envy, you could make a panel to slide up and out when you need it.

Pruning

The general rule of thumb for trees and shrubs that need an annual prune is: if it flowers before midsummer, prune in the autumn; if after midsummer, prune the next spring.

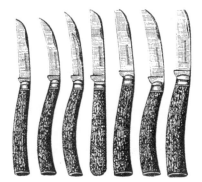

How to make friends and influence plants
Protecting your plants

Plants that help each other:

A mong the most helpful tips to come down to us from the observations and the practical experience of generations of gardeners are those that concern the protective qualities of certain plants. If you plant x near y one will either stimulate or protect the other (see list pp. 43–44). Interestingly, science has in many cases been able to determine why this should be so.

For example:

Marigolds (tagetes)
Although much rarer today, there was a time when all cottage gardens seemed to have marigolds growing everywhere, sometimes even in rows along the front of every border.

In the matter of self-seeding marigolds are not shy and retiring, and this was rarely an accident. Most garden pests hate marigolds because of the excretions from their roots (and the warning emitted by their aroma) which kill eelworm and a variety of other baddies in the soil. French, African and Mexican marigolds all perform this service, and the last is even recommended for controlling ground elder. All vegetables and flowers welcome marigolds growing among them, and potatoes, tomatoes, peas, brassicas and roses seem especially to benefit from their friendly presence.

Foxgloves (digitalis purpurea)
The poor old common foxglove is often the first supposed weed to go on the bonfire when a new garden is being made, or an old one being cleared out, but think before you leap to pull it up! It stimulates growth in the plants around it and helps keep disease at bay, which gave rise to the old saying:

    Grow foxgloves nearby your store of potatoes, tomatoes and apples.

Rhododendrons and azaleas are said particularly to thrive when foxgloves are grown among them, and there is some evidence to support this.

The onion family (onions, chives & garlic – allium)
In the old days there was a widespread habit in the countryside of hanging strings of onions in the house to keep it free of infectious diseases because, it was believed, onions absorbed poisons. Modern science knows that onion and garlic both have the power to prevent blood-clotting and the build-up of cholesterol but, despite much research, has still not pinpointed exactly what gives the onion family its remarkable healing powers.

In the garden, this family performs as well for its fellow plants as it does for human health. Garlic and onion especially have a pungent smell and, like the foxglove, contain repellent as well as stimulating properties.

To keep rabbits away from the crops, it was said, *plant a row of onions, chives or garlic. They will never pass through such a border.*

If Dracula can't cope with garlic, what hope has the humble rabbit? It's also recommended to

Plant garlic and chives among roses to keep greenfly away
and to
Keep pests off raspberries and vines by planting garlic among them

If you boil the leaves of wild garlic in water, you can use this as a spray to repel scale insects and aphids, and prevent tomato blight, bean rust and mildew in cucumbers.

Tips from the
OLD GARDENERS

As an example of the stimulating effects of the onion family, it has always been said that *beetroot and onions agree well together.*

Carrots and onions also help each other along by mutually repelling carrot fly and onion fly.

But although members of the onion family grown amongst most flowers and vegetables act as a powerful deterrent to harmful insects there are, as in most laws of nature, always some unexpected exceptions. Peas and beans seem to dislike having a member of the onion family anywhere near them – rather like politicians of different persuasions preferring opposite sides of the House of Commons.

Lavender
Lavender is still popular in the home today, if only as a fragrance. But for a great many years it had a practical as well as sweet-smelling purpose Before the advent of artificial fibres, little

muslin bags of lavender were stored with linen and in wardrobes to keep away moths and other insects. It was also the practice in many houses to soak a ball of cotton wool in lavender and hang it in a muslin bag to keep flies away. (It used to be said that lavender oil was a cure for lice and worms in dogs and cats, but as I've never had the heart to send my old dog out to meet his pals in a seductive cloud of lavender I cannot report any personal experience of this.) It being but a short step to the garden, it's perhaps not surprising that there too it has decorative, odorous and deterrent benefits.

As with garlic, lavender is a deterrent to some of the harmful insects (but happily not bees), and *lavender planted among roses keeps the aphids away.*

So if you don't fancy trying garlic next to your roses, you have an alternative.

Tips from the
OLD GARDENERS

Gardening folklore overflows with tips about plants which benefit from each other's company.

A handful are quoted here, but after a while they become confusing to follow, so in the hope that you won't toss this book out of the window in frustration, there is a table of likes and dislikes on pp. 43–44.

Peas and beans do well in the company of carrots, leeks and turnips.
and
Potatoes do well when planted close to peas and beans
(the latter contain nitrates which are beneficial to potatoes)

To protect cucumbers from wireworm, push a fresh carrot into the soil near each plant.

Tips from the
OLD GARDENERS

Thyme is a good companion plant to the cabbage.
but
Strawberries and cabbages are not best friends.
however
Plant strawberries near borage, beans and lettuces for their mutual benefit. (you're probably beginning to see what I mean)

Basil grown amongst tomatoes keeps whitefly away.

Parsley grown among roses increases their scent.

On the subject of parsley there are all sorts of interesting, not to say strange, sayings:

Always sow parsley from seed, and never, never move it — *move parsley, move your wife*, according to an old French tradition!

Also, *it takes an honest man to grow parsley!* Is that so! Those of you who've jumped that hurdle will still need to take care, because: *the man who grows parsley will have no sons and his daughters will be barren.* To the male mind, there is an answer.

Clearly, the woman of the house must sow the parsley. Since another piece of folklore solemnly pronounces that where parsley grows well it is the man of the house who wears the trousers, it all starts to look like a well-hatched plot to ensure it's the wife who's pushed out into the garden, in the pouring rain no doubt, to do the gardening!

On a more cheerful note, though, if you're addicted to garlic but still want people to talk to you at a party, chew some parsley first. And do you know why we garnish so many things with parsley? Because it's an antidote to poison, so we used to put it on our guests' food as a sign that, although our cooking might not be up to scratch, we weren't trying to bump them off.

This little table may help you to see at a glance some of the plants which help others by being grown close by (with a third column to sound a warning bell where there is a pet hate!)

Plant/vegetable	Helps	Does not like
Marigolds	Cabbage family, Peas, Potatoes, Tomatoes	
Thyme	Cabbage family	Potatoes
Parsley	Beans, Carrots, Asparagus, Turnips, Tomatoes	
Asparagus	Tomatoes, Parsley	Onion family
Beans	Carrots, Peas, Courgettes, Leeks, Turnips, Parsley, Strawberries	
Beetroot	Onion family	
Cabbage family	Thyme	Onion family, Strawberries

Plant/vegetable	Helps	Does not like
Carrots	Beans, Peas, Leeks, Lettuce, Turnips, Onion family	
Courgettes	Beans, Peas	
Leeks	Beans, Peas, Carrots, Turnips	
Lettuce	Carrots, Strawberries	
Onion family	Carrots, Beetroot	Beans, Peas, Strawberries, Cabbage family
Peas	Beans, Carrots, Leeks Turnips, Courgettes	Onion family
Potatoes	Beans, Peas, Strawberries	Tomatoes
Strawberries	Beans, Lettuce	Cabbage family
Tomatoes	Asparagus, Parsley	Potatoes
Turnips	Beans, Carrots, Leeks, Parsley	

Saving your plants from drowning

Given the uncertainties of the British climate and the excessive rain we sometimes get, some parts of the garden may flood especially if your soil contains a lot of clay. This is bad news for many plants and they may keel over and die as a result. You could overcome this by making raised beds which will allow the excess water to drain away. On the Isle of Skye they call them "lazybeds" but don't be fooled. You'll have to put in a fair share of work.

Dig a trench round the area to be raised and throw the soil from the trench up on to the bed to lift it, say, nine or twelve inches above the surrounding earth. You can always raid the compost heap to help get the level up. If you live on stony ground, you can use the stones you dig out of the trench to face the slopes of the raised bed or, if this makes you feel like a 19th century convict in Australia, you can raid the local garden centre for rocks or cobbles.

But what happens if there's a drought?

As you'll have worked out already, the only problem with a raised bed comes if there's a prolonged dry spell, and the wheeze for draining excessive water results in a bed which dries out faster than anywhere else in the garden. But then how many prolonged dry spells do we get in a normal British summer? Two perhaps, or possibly three?

The answer is watering – of course – but watering the right way. Even a daily five minute soaking for every plant in your garden is not going to do a lot of good. The water may penetrate as much as an inch, but all that will do is cause the hair roots to turn up to the surface looking for moisture where they will shrivel in the daily heat. Plants do not need constant watering from above; they need to be driving their roots down towards the water table below. One *really thorough* watering once a week in a dry spell will do. So why not divide your garden into seven zones, and each evening give one zone a good drenching for at least thirty minutes, giving the water a real chance to sink right down to the bottom of the roots.

A final thought: if, like me, you live on heavy clay and find the soil in your garden bakes hard on top and opens into big cracks in dry weather, keep on breaking up the surface with a hoe or a fork. A hard top surface laced with cracks sets off an underground reaction that causes such moisture as is below to be drawn to the surface and evaporate. If you keep on breaking up the surface and creating a surface layer of dust, it will act like a mulch and help retain moisture.

> *"More and more I am coming to the conclusion that rain is a far more important consideration to a gardener than sun, and that one of the lesser advantages that a gardener gains in life is his thorough enjoyment of a rainy day."*

Margaret Waterfield
1907

Will no one rid me of this turbulent bug?
Tips on pest control

However tranquil and peaceful our gardens may appear to us, there is veritable warfare seething beneath the leaves and among the roots. An army of birds, animals and insects is working with zealous intensity to rob us of flowers or fruits, stems or shoots. These days, there are any number of chemical solutions on offer to us at garden centres and many of them do what they say they will do. But what are the side effects? Sometimes there are none, but there are those who would prefer preventatives that they think are less risky – as long as they work.

Birds

Birds eat slugs and snails, greenfly and a variety of insects you'd sooner be without, and in this respect they are anything but pests.

But: pigeons are fond of cabbages; thrushes and blackbirds adore soft fruits; and the buds of shrubs and fruit trees are high on the must-have list of several species.

So you've a decision to make – do you want to welcome birds or deter them? Three hundred years ago Joseph Addison wrote *"I value my garden more for being full of blackbirds than of cherries, and very frankly give them fruit for their songs"* and I can't improve on that sentiment. But there are a few harmless measures you can take to limit the rewards they purloin from your garden if you're prepared to spend a bit of time on them.

To protect fruit bushes from birds, tie black thread around them

Birds have difficulty focussing on black thread which makes it hard for them to judge distance. They won't risk tangling with something which may snag their wings and make escape hazardous. Netting is fine (although expensive) as long as it isn't plastic because they can perch on plastic netting and use their beaks to punch entry holes. Black thread can also be used to protect seed beds. Tie it an inch or two above the ground to small sticks placed either side of the bed - birds won't risk being trapped under it.

Make-believe snakes are a quick and easy deterrent to birds, and can be made by cutting off pieces of old hosepipe two to three feet long. Bend them in a couple of places to make a snake shape and leave them in beds around the garden where the birds can see them from the air.

These days you can buy humming tape or wire in garden centres. Stretch this between posts in your garden and the breeze will produce a vibration that deters birds. If you can sneak one of the children's old cassette tapes you might find the tape inside is a good substitute for a humming wire.

Slugs and snails (and a few others)

Finding ways of keeping slugs, snails, caterpillars and the like at bay is a perennial headache for the gardener – and has been back into the distant past. My father saved the soot from the annual sweeping of the chimneys to put round the flower and vegetable beds, and in the days of steam trains slate smeared with soot and engine oil was a recommended recipe. But soot is now a rare commodity (though it did seem to work in its day).

A mulch of oak leaves was another old formula for keeping the slugs and snails away, and a modern version of this is gravel (so it's fortunate that gravel gardens are popular these days) or bark chippings, because these particular pests dislike passing over rough surfaces. A word of warning if you use bark, though. Go for the coarser, larger bark rather than the small chippings which are relatively smooth, so less of a deterrent (and in any case are more quickly absorbed into the soil).

Many old professional gardeners in the large houses would put jam jars full of salt water at strategic points round the garden. Any slugs, snails, caterpillars or other pests they found in doing their daily work would be popped straight into the jar. Since slugs can't stand salt, seaweed straight from the seashore (should you happen to live

near it) is an excellent deterrent – but don't put it too near the plants because, potatoes apart, they can't stand it either.

An old but still familiar (and effective) solution is to place saucers of lightly diluted beer close to the plants you want to protect. The slugs and snails will slither in and meet a happy end, provided the beer is bitter and not lager. Whatever else they may be, slugs and snails are not lager louts, and will keep their olfactory organs resolutely turned up if the beer is not the real thing.

Hostas come under particularly heavy attack from slugs and snails, and a tip for giving them some extra protection is to pot

---

"We have descended into the garden and caught three hundred slugs. How I love the mixture of the beautiful and the squalid in gardening. It makes it so like life."

Evelyn Underhill
1912

---

the hostas, and then dig them into the garden with the rim of the pots an inch or two above the surface of the surrounding soil. Grease the rim of the pot well with petroleum jelly, and put grit or fine gravel around the plant itself. In the unlikely event that the slug or snail makes it over the slippery rim, the grit should make him think life is thoroughly unfair.

All these things help to deter, but slugs and snails outnumber us and our plants pretty heavily, so we will always be fighting a rearguard action. All the more reason then to encourage into our gardens the birds, black beetles, hedgehogs, toads and other allies that like nothing more than a starter of slug with a main course of snail.

Moles

Ah yes, moles. I was rather hoping you wouldn't ask. Are they pests or are they friends? After all, they don't eat your plants — they're after insects and grubs, which is a help.

To be sure, they sometimes tunnel right under your plants and damage the roots and, the big sin, they *make molehills on your lawn!* But even this has advantages. Not only do mole runs help the drainage, but molehills are a wonderful source of beautifully

mixed up nutrients carefully brought to the surface as nice loose soil by the co-operative mole, all ready for you to scoop up and use beneficially in seed beds or other parts of your garden. The grass will regrow quickly enough afterwards, so why take it out on the mole? If you must, be assured that nobody has found a solution, ancient or modern, which everyone will swear is effective, despite centuries of trying! It might just be that moles are smarter than us.

Tips from the
OLD GARDENERS

Of the remedies which have, at least, some supporters, you could try:

Stuffing mothballs or Jeyes fluid, both of which smell vile to moles, into the galleries connecting the molehills. You will need good, old-fashioned camphor mothballs as many modern ones use chemical substitutes.

Planting *euphorbia lathyrus* or *euphorbia lactea* in the garden – again, they detest the smell;

Smoking them out with so-called mole bombs pushed down into the galleries;

Sinking empty bottles (neck above ground) in the galleries. The breeze blowing over the necks is reckoned to create a booming effect which might persuade the moles they've tunnelled into the middle of Heathrow.

Finally, if you've got lots and lots of time, and you're celebrated for your patience, you could sit in a deckchair waiting for the magic moment when you see a molehill going up. Treading softly, push a spade down as far as it will go behind the molehill, quickly lever it up and you should find yourself the proud possessor of a real mole. Pop it in a handy sack (which naturally you've got all ready) leap into your car, drive several miles into the country and release it. It will probably find its way back to you years later, but you'll be older and wiser by then.

"The worst enemyes to Gardens are Moles, Catts, Earewiggs, Snailes and Mice, and they must be carefully destroyed, or all your labor is lost."

Sir Thomas Hanmer, 1589

Flies

They don't do much damage to the garden itself, but are a thorough nuisance buzzing around you when you're on all fours in a flower bed, particularly when one of them decides the inside of your ear is the most interesting place on earth.

To repel them grab a few leaves of mint (best of all is peppermint (*mentha piperita*) from which menthol is distilled) and rub them over your face, hands and neck. On the kind of hot day which flies adore this has the added advantage of making the skin feel cool.

A window box of *mentha piperita* at your kitchen window is also a good way of discouraging flies from coming in to see if what you're cooking is the very thing they fancy.

Useful home-grown weapons against pests and other nuisances

There are various plants or substances which can be obtained easily with which to arm yourself in the eternal battle against pests and diseases. Some of them have been mentioned already but are repeated here as a reminder.

Aphids (tiny sap-sucking insects of almost any colour, but greenfly, blackfly and whitefly are the most commonly known):

- Soak nettles in water for a few days, draw off the liquid through a sieve and use as a spray;

- Boil wild garlic leaves in water and use the resulting liquid as a spray;
- Grow chives, garlic or lavender among roses to keep aphids away;
- Push twigs of the elder tree in the ground around broad beans to keep off blackfly;
- Grow basil around tomatoes to protect the latter from whitefly.
- Soak rhubarb leaves in rainwater (say a pound of leaves in two pints of water) for about four weeks and use the liquid as a spray for fruit trees in leaf (but not once the fruit is growing). Rhubarb contains oxalic acid and kills most insects attracted to fruit trees, but it is also toxic to humans so keep the liquid labelled as a reminder of what it is, and out of the way of children or anyone who might be tempted to try and drink it.

- If you failed to earth up your potatoes properly you are likely to have a few green ones sticking up above the soil. The greener they are the more poisonous, and you can make an insect-killing spray from them. If you boil about half a dozen green potatoes in a medium sized saucepan the water, drawn off, will make your spray.

- Nothing to do with aphids, but on the subject of potatoes, the water you boil your potatoes in before the meal makes a good path cleaner. So if your paths are beginning to look soiled and careworn, don't tip the potato water down the sink, pour it on the path!

Carrot fly:
- Grow onions among your carrots to keep carrot fly away;

- If you detest onions, break up a mothball and sow it in the drill with the carrot seeds;
- Or do both.

Cabbage root fly and carrot fly:
- Take a little dry sand, shake a few drops of paraffin into it and mix. Then sprinkle the sand alongside the plants to deter the insect from laying eggs. You will need to do this on a regular basis, and to renew after rain. A little and often is the rule.

Club root (which affects cabbages and brassicas):
- Take some rhubarb stalks, cut into short lengths and push one into the soil alongside each cabbage. The oxalic acid protects against club root;
- But with or without rhubarb stalks, ensure your cabbage patch is well drained to discourage the mould that causes club root.

Cabbage white fly:
- Plant marigolds (tagetes) among the rows.

Mildew:
- If a mildew problem develops in your cabbages or sprouts, use a spray of methylated spirits;
- Mildew in roses can be treated with a sprinkling of sulphur in powder or dust form;
- Mildew on gooseberry leaves is a common problem. If you pour some boiling water onto a few chives and let them soak for a little, you can wipe the liquid onto the gooseberry leaves to get rid of the mildew;
- The liquid left after boiling wild garlic leaves can be used as a spray to prevent mildew on cucumbers.

"There is nothing more unpleasant than to tell anyone suffering under a calamity that there is no tangible remedy; but it is infinitely better to do so than delude them with a false one."

Peter Henderson
1874

Protecting fruit trees from attack

- An old piece of advice is to grow trailing or climbing nasturtiums round the trunks, or grow lavender beneath the trees. They will, it is said, repel troublesome insects and encourage fruitfulness;

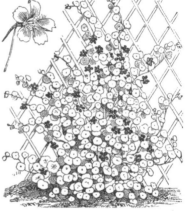

- Cottage gardeners used to hang branches of elder among the boughs of their fruit trees (and among their cabbages) to keep insects away;

- It is said that apple blight can be tackled by hanging a dead tomato plant in its branches over the winter. Also that the smoke from burning old tomato plants below the tree will fumigate it;

- To prevent the larvae of codling moth from ruining your apple crop, tie strips of corrugated cardboard (smooth side out) round the trunks of the trees in the latter part of the summer, say July. The larvae will hibernate in the little tubes and ridges of the cardboard, so first thing in the new year, cut the cardboard off and have a bonfire.

- A frequently-quoted remedy against leaf curl in fruit (mainly peach) trees is to hang clusters of mothballs in the branches. This is so often recommended that it must work!

Wasps

It's a moot point if the wasp is a friend or an enemy because there's a lot of the Jekyll and Hyde in him. He's very useful in the fight against insects, and accounts for huge numbers before about August, at which point he shows his fatal weakness of a very sweet tooth. Then he becomes an irritant to humans, buzzing about otherwise relaxed picnic parties looking for jam, lemonade, beer and so on.

This may be all right for the majority, since wasps don't sting unless attacked or provoked beyond waspish endurance, and their stings (which contain little toxin) cause only a small reaction.

Unfortunately, the wasp's passion for sweet things leads him straight to the fruit tree, and to protect our fruit means some awkward scrambling about hanging jam jars on the branches. The key to success is what is in the jars of course.

Our old friend beer is high on the list of things that will attract wasps. A little jam or honey covered with water (enough to drown in), or sugared water, are alternatives

if you happen to have a teetotal nest in your garden. In each case the jar needs to be about a quarter full, and for an average tree you will need two or three jars tied round the neck with string or twine and hung from different branches.

Weeds and things

An old country rhyme goes like this:

Cut thistles in May, they grow in a day;
Cut them in June, that is too soon;
Cut them in July, then they die.

Indeed, if you live near meadows that have a heavy growth of thistles in the summer, you may see the farmer come out in July and cut them, leaving them to dry and wither in the sun.

This is because by July the seed heads are well formed but not yet ready to be dispersed, and if you cut them in July it's too late for the plant to grow again in time to make new seed heads – or so at least the theory goes. In practice they need to be cut again at the end of August.

All of which may be interesting, but very few of us have gardens big enough to justify worry about the optimum time for thistle-cutting. We just pull up the odd one or two that settle in our blessed plot and worry about the more pernicious little blighters.

My father's garden was afflicted with couch grass, and although he was a patient and long-suffering man couch grass could rouse him to a passion that would seem incredible to anyone not similarly afflicted. Folk wisdom says that *a thick sowing of turnip seed will rid the land of couch*, and sayings along these lines crop up so often that there are certainly grounds for trying it.

As for ground elder ... front row rugby forwards, celebrated over many a pint for their endurance and fortitude, have been known to break down and weep when afflicted by ground elder. Mexican marigold is reputed to control this pestilence. I cannot guarantee that it works, but it might be worth a try if only for a few months relief while you wait to find out.

Mulching to keep the weeds away

The snag is you have to pull them all up first but, having done so, mulching – i.e. spreading a layer of something over the soil – will make it difficult for more weeds to germinate and come through. As weeds are the real street urchins of the plant world, able to flourish in the most surprising places, this is a worthwhile objective and it has the double benefit of conserving moisture (or protecting against frost) which your "proper" plants will thank you for.

Grass cuttings are the simplest and most easily available mulch but, depending on where you live, you may have a nearby supply of seaweed, straw or bracken all of which can be used as a mulch. So too can leafmould (see p. 30) which is a good mulch as well as a good manure.

But there are a few words of warning about these different materials. Grass cuttings, leafmould and seaweed are all rich in nitrogens so they enrich the soil as they rot. But seaweed should be washed and dried before use to get rid of the salt, which will otherwise be harmful to many plants. Seaweed and leafmould remain cool as they rot down; whereas grass cuttings heat up and should not be put too near shallow rooted plants such as azaleas. In general, it is important not to put any mulch straight on top of dry soil. If there's been no rain for a while, water the soil well (and if you're using a mulch of straw, make sure that it is old, moist and starting to rot, not young and dry).

"An unmulched garden looks to me like some naked thing which, for one reason or another, would be better off with clothes on."

Ruth Stout
1971

A weed that runs to seed is a seven-year seed, it is said, as proof that weeds not only distribute their seeds in huge quantities but do so with irresponsible abandon using a variety of cunning mechanisms which even Baldrick would have envied. I mention this just to stiffen your resolve to have a good mulching campaign preceded by a thorough weeding assault.

Weeds in gravel paths

Don't despair. Just pop round to your local cigarette factory for some sweepings off the floor, mix with ashes from the bonfire you're not allowed to light any more, add some salt and sprinkle on the affected parts. Bingo. Alternatively, resign yourself to pulling them by hand.

If all else fails ...

If nothing works, and you're considering having a nervous breakdown as a means of escape from the uneven struggle against pests, you could try planting a rosemary bush. In the old days it was grown in most gardens to keep witches away and bring good luck. If it is less effective than expected, and a multi-seater broomload of witches turns up at the garden gate you can always whip up a brew of rosemary tea which is reputed to soothe digestive disorders. Even if they don't want it, you may well need it.

Better still, Gerard's famous *Herball*, written in 1597, said that rosemary *comforteth the cold, weak and feeble brain in a most wonderful manner!* Maybe that's why many of the most prominent people in ancient Rome wore garlands of rosemary around their necks.

Houseleeks grown on the roof or in the crevices of house walls were also supposed to protect the home from ill fortune – and lightning strikes! Speaking for myself, I don't think I'll risk it.

The next round's on me!
Encouraging friends into the garden

What's a pest and who's a friend?

The rule of thumb – but as usual there are exceptions – is it's a friend if it scuttles away quickly; it's an enemy if it's slow and sluggish.

Exceptions: earthworms move slowly but are friends – good friends. They bring soil to the surface, help to oxygenate it and generally assist in mixing up the nutrients (as moles do, but as their holes are bigger we're less forgiving.)

Earwigs move quickly, but they are herbivorous and eat your plants – especially dahlias. A useful way of trapping them is to put a little straw in a small flower pot or jam jar and invert it on the top of the pole supporting your plant. Earwigs will nestle down in the straw and you can dispose of them next morning as the mood takes you. That at least is the theory. It does work, but insects sometimes seem to have animal cunning and they won't all fight each other for the privilege of being first in the trap.

Apart from birds, hedgehogs and earthworms, your special friends in the garden are centipedes, spiders, ladybirds, lacewings, black beetles, hoverflies and toads, which uncomplainingly devote nearly all their time to stripping your garden of soil and plant pests, such as aphids. If you're lucky enough to have a good population of these friends, you won't often need to bother the garden centre for pesticides.

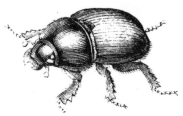

Hedgehogs

Since we've mentioned them, did you know that hedgehogs have been around, pretty much as we know them today, for about 15 million years? Although they eat earthworms (who are friends, but fortunately reproduce at a greater rate than the average hedgehog can keep up with) they have a great appetite for slugs and caterpillars, so are well worth encouraging. You don't need to do anything for them in the summer except to avoid leaving litter such as empty baked bean tins around – hedgehogs have been known to get stuck in them trying to reach that last little lick at the bottom. But in the autumn they're preparing to hibernate and need all the body fat they can grow to help them survive. So on October nights a saucer of pet food with a few crumbled dog biscuits, and a bowl of drinking water, will give them a balanced diet – provided you can stop Fido getting there first, of course. And if you have a bonfire any time between November and March, it's worth shaking up the pile before you light it to ensure they're not hibernating in it.

Toads

Toads are also good news, since they do sterling work in decimating the pest population. The way to encourage them is to have a pond in your garden, but if you don't want the bother of a pond a nice boggy and damp place will do since, like Eeyore, toads find this a good habitat. But if you have a pond with steep sides, do make sure there's a ladder or ramp for them to climb out. They can't gorge on your slugs and snails if they're stuck at the bottom with the water lilies.

Encouraging friendly insects into your garden

There are two basic ways of doing this, though one may make you take a deep breath first. If you want to attract those nice friendly insects that gobble up the nasties, they've got to be persuaded there are enough nasties to make their journey worthwhile.

Tips from the
OLD GARDENERS

For the first way, we're back to those ubiquitous nettles, I'm afraid. The big patch of nettles that I recommended near the start of this book will grow early in the year and by the start of Spring will have a supply of aphids which the predatory insects will follow. If you cut the nettles back in, say, mid Spring, the predators will hunt further afield and scour your other garden plants of naughty old aphids.

The second way of attracting the better class of insect is, of course, to grow the plants they like best. There are lists of these in many gardening books, but they include alyssum, anemone, arabis, campanula, erigeron, eryngium, gazania, geranium, geum, gypsophila, helianthus, liatris, nicotania, papaver, rudbeckia, salvia, scabious, stachys and veronica.

What have you got?
Well don't come near me then.
Some plants that heal

"The powre of herbes, both which can hurt and ease"

Edmund Spenser 1552–99

Herbal remedies have a history stretching back four thousand years to the ancient Egyptians. Even today, if you are walking at dawn in the hills above, say, Beirut in the Lebanon you may well meet a villager gathering healing plants and herbs.

In Britain, our knowledge of healing plants developed in the Physic Gardens of convents and monasteries in the early Middle Ages. Centuries ago, the monks and nuns were the only doctors. They grew the herbs, or medicines, themselves and discovered their healing properties by trial, error and close observation. Many of the plants they then thought of as medicinal herbs, we now think of as flowers (or weeds) in our cultivated gardens.

As time went on, some of the wisdom of the monks was acquired by those who called themselves physicians, or others who sometimes were regarded as witches. Both would have used the same plants, but the quantities and the amount of dilution used could represent the difference between healing and harm. For example two of the most powerful plants which witches were said to use were deadly nightshade (*atropa belladonna*) and henbane (*hypocamus niger*), and yet belladonna can be found – in minute quantities – in a great many modern medicines, and today "hyoscine" (a preparation using a small amount of henbane) is used by women in childbirth and those suffering from nervous disorders.

Perhaps the bad reputation of so-called "black" witches arose less from malevolence and more from an inadequate command of the skills needed in using herbs for healing. Which is a warning that this section of the book is not intended as a medical guide, nor is it to be used as a do-it-yourself manual!

Apples

An apple a day keeps the doctor away
and
To eat an apple going to bed will make the doctor beg his bread

Apple remedies abound in folklore. For example, the juice of the apple was said to cure cuts. Modern research has found that pectin is present in apples, and as pectin has germicidal properties there could be more than a grain, or pip, of truth in the old sayings.

Borage

Juice taken from the leaves of borage and made into a syrup with sugar or honey expels melancholy and sadness, clarifies the blood and comforts the heart.

All that from a flower we often regard as a weed? Ever since the Romans were in Britain, we've attributed powers to borage that border on the miraculous. In its time it's been an antidote to bites and stings, ringworm and yellow jaundice, and has even been recommended to young ladies as a cure for swooning and unrequited love.

Is this why we use it today as a garnish for a glass of Pimms?

Alas, the truth is more prosaic. Borage flowers contain potassium nitrate, a soluble crystalline salt that has a cooling property useful not just in gunpowder and for curing meat, but to add a cool flavour to many kinds of drink.

Basil: (ocimum basilicum)

Talking of parties – or at least alcoholic drinks – basil is an excellent thing to have to hand. Basil is a nerve tonic that is also a stimulant and it settles the stomach, preventing nausea and vomiting. Since it's also used as a garnish on food and can be safely eaten, it's a good tip to eat a leaf or two before the party gets under way. Four hundred years ago, basil used to be given as a token of friendship.

Castor Oil Plant: (ricinus communis)

A handsome plant for the conservatory, and the bane of children for generations. In the 16th and 17th centuries the plant was thought to be good for bruises, burns, scars and easing the pains of rheumatism; dropsy, gout and sciatica; and to improve hearing. Is that all, I can almost hear you ask.

It was about four hundred years ago that adults decided there was no reason for their children to escape the infliction of castor oil, and casting about for a plausible reason decided it was just the thing to cure worms. After all, a worm was about as likely to welcome castor oil as a politician to welcome a tax cut. For later generations – indeed right up to the present day – dosing with castor oil was recommended by everyone except the children themselves as a preventative for winter colds and snuffles. The kids would probably have preferred the colds and snuffles.

Celandine: (ranunculus ficaria)

It was once called pilewort (wort is old english for a plant or root, and appears in many old plant names). Need I go on? Yes, you're quite right, it was once used to cure piles. Luckily, that belief didn't last long and the lesser celandine relapsed into its comfortable anonymity somewhere between a weed and a rock garden plant, waiting for Wordsworth to celebrate it in verse.

Comfrey: (symphytum officianale)

When you see "officianale" or "officianalis" in the latin name of a plant it indicates a pedigree established in the monastic physic garden.

The moistened, pulped root of comfrey, applied to a broken arm or leg, set like plaster and therefore hastened the knitting of the bone. It is said this knowledge was brought back to England by soldiers returning from the Crusades, and among the traditional names for comfrey are Saracens Root, Knitbone and Boneset.

Cowslip: (primula veris)

Cowslip tea was – and, I believe, still is by quite a lot of people – used to soothe headaches and nervous tension, and to counteract insomnia.

83

Daisy (bellis perennis)

The daisy has a golden eye surrounded by petals which close at night and reopen by day – hence the old name *days-eye*, celebrated by Chaucer, Milton, Shakespeare and the indefatigable Wordsworth.

Four hundred years ago the daisy was admitted to the garden as a welcome flower (and now regards the best bits of the lawn as its birthright), but even before that it was known as a healing plant. Called *bruisewort*, a poultice of leaves was considered excellent for alleviating pain and treating bumps and bruises – as it still is, being one of the great homeopathic remedies. The flowers and leaves of the daisy contain quantities of oil and ammoniacal salts, so if you stamp on the leaves and press them to a bruise or swelling it will respond quickly and well.

Feverfew: (tanacetum parthenium)

This is a plant that has had pride of place in herb gardens for two thousand years. Although it was introduced to Britain when the Romans were building everything in straight lines, the name is from the old French "febrifuge" meaning to drive away fever, and that is exactly what the monks used it for. It was taken as a cold cure mixed with honey, or used as a gargle for sore throats. Later on it was believed that pushing some feverfew leaves up your nose would help cure a migraine, and since modern science has made so little progress in the matter, maybe it's still worth a shot.

Apart from its herbal uses, feverfew is a pretty plant and has been grown in the garden for its flowers since the 16th century. Later, the Victorians began to cultivate varieties for bedding and today you can choose dwarf varieties for the rock garden or larger ones for herbaceous beds.

Foxglove: (digitalis purpurea)

The old herbalists thought foxgloves a cure-all for almost any human health problem. In his famous *Herball*, Gerard recommended it as a cure for falling sickness, fevers, agues, liver complaints, suppurating wounds and for "cleaning the body of clammy and naughty humours". Phew! But towards the end of the 18th century the foxglove began to be used in the treatment of heart complaints, being the source of the drug digitalis, extracted from the leaves. As with belladonna and henbane, the foxglove is full of harmful toxins as well as producing digitalis, so it's not a plant to be messed with.

Houseleek: (sempervivum)

"If some mouse, spider, fly, wasp, hornet or other venomous beast has by its bite or sting raised a lump on your flesh, rub the injured part gently with the juice of a houseleek and immediately the pain and the swelling will be assuaged." If it was good enough for the 16th century, who are we to argue?

Mallow
(malva sylvestris)

If you suffer from boils (in the Duchy of Cornwall you may prefer to refer to them as carbuncles) you could try boiling the leaves and stems of mallow and mixing the juice with bread to make a poultice for wrapping around the affected spots. Well, it was only a suggestion. But in the old days they swore by it.

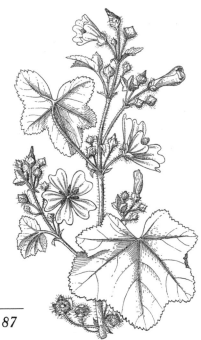

Tips from the
OLD GARDENERS

Marjoram: (origanum vulgare)

If you "are given to overmuch sighing" take the leaves of marjoram, boiled in water and, according to Gerard's *Herball*, all will be well again. It was also recommended for indigestion, earache, insomnia, loss of appetite and dropsy. No wonder you are sighing overmuch.

Nettles: (urtica urens)

Here's the good old stinging nettle again. Would you believe that in addition to being good for currant bushes, for the compost heap, for liquid manure and for attracting insects it's also good for treating stings and superficial burns? To lay it on even thicker, in the country they used to make sheets and tablecloths out of nettle stalks, and swore they were harder wearing than linen.

In Scotland, they still make soup from nettles, and you may well find it on the menu of some upmarket restaurants. In Jersey, nettle tea was reckoned an excellent remedy for pleurisy, wheezing and shortness of breath.

The hairs of the stinging nettle contain histamine and acetylcholine, and on the good homeopathic principle that like treats like, a tincture of urtica urens is an excellent thing to apply if you suffer a first degree burn – for instance from a steaming kettle or a hot stove – or a bee sting. Needless to say, the secret is in the dilution, so definitely do not try rubbing a nettle leaf on a sting or burn!

By now you may be so impressed with the powers of the nettle that you're falling a little in love with it. If you get too close and, as loved ones occasionally do, get stung, rub the sting with the leaf of a dock, potato or tomato, or with onion juice.

Pot marigold: (calendula officianalis)

Calendula was another of those plants which the old herbalists considered a cure for all ills — jaundice, toothache, bee stings and warts to name a few.

This may be overstating the case but calendula is nevertheless a remarkable plant, and a major weapon in the armoury of the modern homeopathic doctor, by whom it is regarded as the remedy excelling all others for healing open cuts without resort to stitching. As it cleans the wound as well as repairs it, it's a wonderful thing to have handy, especially with active children liable at any moment to graze a knee on steps or gravel. Luckily tubes of calendula ointment can be bought from many chemists.

If you prefer it as a cordial drink, pour a pint of boiling water over two handfuls of leaves and flowers. Apart from healing cuts and inflammations, it is good for the heart and circulation.

Rose of Sharon/St Johns Wort: (hypericum calycinum)

St Johns Wort used also to be known by an old French name of *Tutsan*, from "tout" and "sain" meaning to heal all (Rose of Sharon is a fairly modern name, being used only since 1864). It was used to cure ulcers, internal bleeding, internal and external wounds, and old sores.

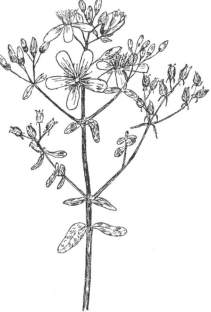

As we've already seen, some of the old folk wisdom makes improbably comprehensive claims about the virtues of some healing plants, whereas in other cases they were impressively accurate. This is one of the accurate claims. Three hundred years ago, Culpeper noted that hypericum "opens obstructions and dissolves swellings" and the dear old chap wasn't far out.

Today it's used by homeopaths for abscesses and injuries to the nerves – for example, if you shut your fingers in the car door, or fall heavily on the base of your spine. You can buy hypericum tincture in homeopathic chemists and use it externally on such injuries by diluting it 50/50 with lukewarm water.

Sage: (salvia officianalis)

Eat sage in May, and you'll live for aye

Tips from the
OLD GARDENERS

This is a saying that's been around for centuries, but though sage is a remarkable herb, the old wives who predicted living for ever would have had more disgruntled customers than Railtrack — if only they'd lived to complain. Indeed, John Evelyn the 17th century diarist said rather sarcastically that sage seemed to have so many astonishing properties he wondered only that man was not yet immortal.

Salvia comes from the Latin "salvere" meaning to make safe or well. Sage is an antiseptic and astringent, and its leaves have been used to treat headaches and colds, sore throats, aching muscles, epilepsy, lethargy, menstruation problems and liver complaints. Even into living memory it was used as a tooth cleaner, to be rubbed into gums and teeth for removing stains and sweetening the breath.

Like some of the other plants that have beneficial properties for human beings, sage is not popular in the insect world. If you're working in the garden on a summer evening when the gnats and midges are being troublesome, try sticking some sprigs of sage in your clothing or behind your ears and they'll probably leave you in peace (although I can't vouch for the hardy tartan midges north of the border).

It's also a strong aromatic herb used in salads, soups, pickles, cheeses, desserts, vinegars, wines, liqueurs and ales. Indeed, in the view of Henry VIII's subjects, the leaves were good to eat when fried in batter, and better still washed down with a glass of sage beer. Good health and delicacy all in one – the goal of modern man!

Salvia sclarea (clary): a diffusion of its seeds and leaves has been used as a wash for inflamed or sore eyes since mediaeval days – hence the popular name of "clear eyes" – "clary" for short.

Sweet alyssum: (lobularia maritima)

Madwort takes away your anger

Madwort is the common name of sweet alyssum. It was said to have the power of suppressing irritation and bad temper, and so presumably has sedative properties. Science has yet to get to the bottom of this one, but in the stresses and strains of 21st century life maybe we should put pressure on the scientists to speed up their efforts – and if the pressure gets to them they can always chew a leaf of madwort to keep them on the job.

Yarrow: (achillea)

This plant was named after Homer's hero of the Trojan Wars, Achilles, who was reputed to have bound up his soldiers wounds with yarrow to help stop the bleeding. As a result it acquired several popular names, such as bloodwort, staunchweed and soldiers woundwort. Modern research has established that yarrow does indeed contain blood-clotting chemicals.

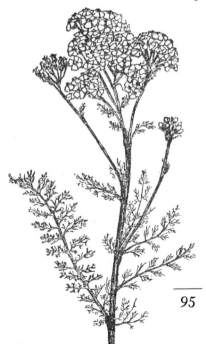

Until quite recently it was recommended to have a handful or two of yarrow leaves handy in the tool shed in case of cuts, and even to bind yarrow round the handles of your gardening tools. Yarrow is another of those plants grown here and there in the old garden because it improved the scent and performance of surrounding plants.

On the other hand, yarrow was said to be a cure for baldness, which strains one's credulity just a little. If you're determined to try anything for the sake of even the wispiest hair, then pick and wash a couple of handfuls of flowers and leaves, pour boiling water over them and leave to stand for half an hour. Rub the liquid on the bald patch – and let me know if you have any luck! But before you dream of making a fortune, first ask yourself why, being surrounded by this miracle plant, so many men throughout history have remained so shiningly bald.